Only This Step

Haiku

by

Philip Kenney

Finishing Line Press
Georgetown, Kentucky

Only This Step

Haiku

Copyright © 2023 by Philip Kenney
ISBN 979-8-88838-096-3 First Edition
All rights reserved under International and Pan-American Copyright Conventions. No part of this book may be reproduced in any manner whatsoever without written permission from the publisher, except in the case of brief quotations embodied in critical articles and reviews.

Publisher: Leah Huete de Maines
Editor: Christen Kincaid
Cover Art: Alamy Stock photos
Author Photo: Pitinan Piyavatin
Cover Design: Elizabeth Maines McCleavy

Order online: www.finishinglinepress.com
also available on amazon.com

Author inquiries and mail orders:
Finishing Line Press
PO Box 1626
Georgetown, Kentucky 40324
USA

For Lori

The Inspiration:

A cicada shell;
it sang itself
utterly away.

Matsuo Basho (1644-1694)
      Translation by Robert Hass

     At the outset of the Pandemic shutdown, many of us thought we would have lots of free time to write, only to find our brains turn to sludge. As time became muddled, so did our thinking. That was my condition in March of 2020 when my plan to resume work on an abandoned novel stalled before it began, thanks to Covid-19 brain.
     Lacking energy and inspiration, I sat before my computer and stared at the empty screen. I asked myself, should I give up on the novel that had haunted me for seven years? Just as I was about to put it back in my desk drawer and forget about writing anything, a little voice in my head said, "Why not have some fun? Write some haiku!" That morning I stopped overthinking and began looking at the world, and next thing I knew two or three haiku were accompanying me home from my regular morning walk.
     This collection is a sampling of the 159 haiku I wrote from early March through mid-June 2020 when, to my surprise, the novel began to beckon. Many of these poems do not strictly follow the 5-7-5 syllabic structure of formal haiku, but I trust they are faithful to its spirit.

Enjoy,

Philip

My hand is empty
 no cup, no victory—
  only this step, and this one

Invocation

Little bird,
you will never be
a soloist

Little bird,
you will never
sing the aria

Your song
will not open
a tulip's heart

but still
little bird, look—
you capture me

Come,
little bird,
sing with me

Woodpecker drumming—
the old Zen Master
wakes from his nap

Yesterday dropped
by again today, this time
I heard the doorbell ring

The silent windchime,
lonely for one sweet caress—
waiting in stillness

Streets are deserted
people huddle in their huts—
a hush comes over

Each Spring a rebirth,
each morning another blossom
dies in full splendor

Light grows eager
for April's bloom—
squirrels leap and climb

    I went looking
        for one and found
    ten thousand!

        I live now
    on the edge,
        of dangling leaves

       Trees
   don't argue
    with wind

       A family of leaves
   holding to a falling twig
        twirl to the ground

>   I find I hurry
>   and make noise—
>   even with this

>   Sit down on the ground,
> be still as the blue heron—
>   why stir all that dust?

> Now, you are golden,
> your breath, the rose of rosemary—
> Light kneels at your feet

> The elder Oak reaches north,
> baby squirrels find a balance beam—
> Me? I sit and stare, aimlessly

I rise and I walk
beneath trees, while raindrops fall—
one leaf, to another

Cool air glides
over my skin—
rippling light on the pond

I adore the language
of knowing, that drifts past
like a misting mirage

The splendid crow,
proud in his black satin suit
speaks as he walks

Bird on the wire
greeting the morning
with song

Such a fine day
to forget about
mortality

What a day
for a daydream—
bumblebee floats by

The pots on the porch
are filling with petunias,
and orange marigolds

If I am to die
like bumblebees in a rose—
let mine be Exbury

Silence touches
something in me
I cannot

Look—
and the world
slows

Listen—
and the wind
quiets

    I thought, I wished,
it was a moth, not a leaf,
    drifting by my ear

    Big daddy longlegs,
        you are so magnificent—
    dangling over the void

The goslings vanished
   following the new moon home—
  what a good mamma

My shadow walks
through other shadows—
  going home

    Look there—
and watch yourself
    disappear!

The goslings are gone
   mother and father too—
swallows over the pond

High in swaying treetops
a quartet of cranky crows
wage a bitter dispute

Same old hungry eyes
turning my head round and round—
green algae on the pond

    Photos of snow
        on tree limbs—
            a chill climbs my spine

    It must be here, not hiding,
      waiting in stillness—
         that knowing

I am trying to grasp,
to find in myself,
    the patience of trees

Bare trees—
a sliver of silver moon
peeks through

Am I a shadow? A dream...
look, the stars turned to sapphires
while I slept!

Hummingbird to me—
"taste everything,
        then fly away humming"

I am easily,
so easily, seduced
    by splendor

            There is sunlight
        and dew on rose petals—
            and there is you, aglow

Thunder, low and slow,
rumbling and tumbling up the gorge—
mountains pause to listen

Whispering rain,
trees sway to the music—
children play in puddles

The crooked branches,
pointing in all directions
speak straightforwardly

I'll drink to that
said the sparrow to the cat—
last call, crows the crow

ACKNOWLEDGMENTS

This book would not exist without the wise guidance of friend and poet, John Brehm. John edited and helped select the haiku that fill the pages of *Only This Step*. The haiku were inspired by my morning walks through the magnificent trees of Laurelhurst Park, in Portland, an inspiration if there ever was one. Those walking meditations took on new meaning and a joyfulness after reading Richard Powers' novel, *The Overstory*. That book altered me and the way I see the world. I will always be grateful. Friends don't get enough recognition in acknowledgements, but without Gary, John, Rob and many others, who I am would surely be diminished, as would my writings. Many thanks to the great grandfather of Haiku, Basho, who speaks to me directly from centuries past. And, as always, my heartfelt thanks to my wife, Lori, to whom this book is dedicated. Finally, I want to thank my son, Georgio, whose edits put the polish on these haiku that they deserved.

Philip Kenney became a psychotherapist in 1978 after completing a graduate degree in Counseling Psychology. He began his career working with children and families and developed into a full-time practice working with adults in intensive psychotherapy. In 1992, he completed a post graduate program in psychoanalytic psychotherapy at the Washington D.C. School of Psychiatry. This training fulfilled a lifelong fascination with the dynamics of the psyche.

That fascination with the inner world deepened, when many years later, at the age of 45, poems began landing in his mind like birds in a tree. They came unbidden, and he scribbled them down, often in the middle of the night. It was exhilarating. Following the sage advice of William Stafford, Mr. Kenney wrote a poem a day for ten years. But it took writing his first novel, *Radiance*, to feel like he had truly become an author.

What he loved about a writing practice from the beginning was that it asked him to be awake. It asked that he be attentive to the particulars of the world, both inner and outer, regardless of the circumstances. In time, Mr. Kenney came to realize what a profound impact this was having on the way he lived. The creative spirit had permeated his entire life and become a way of being, transforming living and the practice of creating into something sacred.

www.ingramcontent.com/pod-product-compliance
Lightning Source LLC
Chambersburg PA
CBHW022126090426
42743CB00008B/1028